DK READERS

Level 1

A Day at Greenhill Farm
Truck Trouble
Tale of a Tadpole
Surprise Puppy!
Duckling Days
A Day at Seagull Beach
Whatever the Weather
Busy Buzzy Bee
Big Machines
Wild Baby Animals
A Bed for the Winter
Born to be a Butterfly
Dinosaur's Day
Feeding Time
Diving Dolphin
Rockets and Spaceships
My Cat's Secret
First Day at Gymnastics
A Trip to the Zoo
I Can Swim!
A Trip to the Library
A Trip to the Doctor
A Trip to the Dentist
I Want To Be A Ballerina

Animal Hide and Seek
Submarines and Submersibles
Animals at Home
Let's Play Soccer
Homes around the World
LEGO: Trouble at the Bridge
LEGO: Secret at Dolphin Bay
Star Wars: What is a Wookiee?
Star Wars: Ready, Set, Podrace!
Star Wars: Luke Skywalker's Amazing Story
Star Wars Clone Wars: Watch Out
    for Jabba the Hutt!
Power Rangers Jungle Fury: We are
    the Power Rangers
A Day in the Life of a Builder
A Day in the Life of a Dancer
A Day in the Life of a Firefighter
A Day in the Life of a Teacher
A Day in the Life of a Musician
A Day in the Life of a Doctor
A Day in the Life of a Police Officer
A Day in the Life of a TV Reporter
Gigantes de Hierro *en español*
Crías del mundo animal *en español*

Level 2

Dinosaur Dinners
Fire Fighter!
Bugs! Bugs! Bugs!
Slinky, Scaly Snakes!
Animal Hospital
The Little Ballerina
Munching, Crunching, Sniffing,
    and Snooping
The Secret Life of Trees
Winking, Blinking, Wiggling,
    and Waggling
Astronaut: Living in Space
Twisters!
Holiday! Celebration Days
    around the World
The Story of Pocahontas
Horse Show
Survivors: The Night the Titanic Sank
Eruption! The Story of Volcanoes
The Story of Columbus
Journey of a Humpback Whale
Amazing Buildings
Feathers, Flippers, and Feet
Outback Adventure: Australian Vacation

Sniffles, Sneezes, Hiccups, and Coughs
Ice Skating Stars
Let's Go Riding
I Want to Be a Gymnast
Starry Sky
Earth Smart: How to Take Care
    of the Environment
Water Everywhere
Telling Time
A Trip to the Theater
Journey of a Pioneer
LEGO: Castle Under Attack
LEGO: Rocket Rescue
Star Wars: Journey Through Space
Star Wars: A Queen's Diary
Star Wars: R2-D2 and Friends
Star Wars Clone Wars: Anakin in Action!
MLB: A Batboy's Day
MLB: Let's Go to the Ballpark!
Spider-Man: Worst Enemies
Meet the X-Men
¡Insectos! *en español*
¡Bomberos! *en español*
La Historia de Pocahontas *en español*

A Note to Parents

DK READERS is a compelling program for beginning readers, designed in conjunction with leading literacy experts, including Dr. Linda Gambrell, Distinguished Professor of Education at Clemson University. Dr. Gambrell has served as President of the National Reading Conference, the College Reading Association, and the International Reading Association.

Beautiful illustrations and superb full-color photographs combine with engaging, easy-to-read stories to offer a fresh approach to each subject in the series. Each DK READER is guaranteed to capture a child's interest while developing his or her reading skills, general knowledge, and love of reading.

The five levels of DK READERS are aimed at different reading abilities, enabling you to choose the books that are exactly right for your child:

Pre-level 1: Learning to read
Level 1: Beginning to read
Level 2: Beginning to read alone
Level 3: Reading alone
Level 4: Proficient readers

The "normal" age at which a child begins to read can be anywhere from three to eight years old. Adult participation through the lower levels is very helpful for providing encouragement, discussing storylines, and sounding out unfamiliar words.

No matter which level you select, you can be sure that you are helping your child learn to read, then read to learn!

LONDON, NEW YORK, MUNICH,
MELBOURNE, AND DELHI

Series Editor Deborah Lock
U.S. Editor John Searcy
Art Editor Mary Sandberg
Managing Art Editor Rachael Foster
Production Editor Sean Daly
Production Claire Pearson
Picture Researcher Harriet Mills
Jacket Designer Natalie Godwin

Reading Consultant
Linda Gambrell, Ph.D.

First American Edition, 2009
09 10 11 12 13 10 9 8 7 6 5 4 3
Published in the United States by DK Publishing
375 Hudson Street, New York, New York 10014

Copyright © 2009 Dorling Kindersley Limited

DK books are available at special discounts when purchased
in bulk for sales promotions, premiums,
fund-raising, or educational use.
For details, contact: DK Publishing Special Markets
375 Hudson Street, New York, New York 10014
SpecialSales@dk.com

A catalog record for this book is available
from the Library of Congress
ISBN: 978-0-7566-4522-9 (Paperback)
ISBN: 978-0-7566-4523-6 (Hardcover)

Color reproduction by Colourscan, Singapore
Printed and bound in China by L. Rex Printing Co. Ltd.

The publisher would like to thank the following for their kind
permission to reproduce their photographs:
(Key: a-above; b-below/bottom; c-center; l-left; r-right; t-top)
Alamy Images: John Angerson 28b; Paul Collis 8-9 (main image);
Danita Delimont 9tr, 12-13, 25tr, 32tl; Franck Fotos 31cr; JTB Photo
Communications, Inc/Haga Library 16-17; Tom Mackie 26-27; Jeff
Morgan alternative technology 23tr; Photofusion Picture Library 3c;
The Photolibrary Wales 10-11, 11tr, 13cla; Robert Harding Picture
Library Ltd 13tr; Henry Westheim Photography 14, 15tr. **Corbis:** Jean
Pierre Amet/Sygma 30; Bob Krist 20-21 (main image); Benedict
Luxmoore/Arcaid 29; **Getty Images:** Jeremy Horner/Riser 17t;
Photonica/Franco Zecchin 7bl, 32clb; Stuart Westmorland/Stone 24-25.
Imagestate: Goran Burenhult 18cl, 32cl. **naturepl.com:** Eric Baccega 6,
7, 35br; Constantinos Petrinos 18-19 (main image), 19tr. **Robert Estall
Photo Library:** Carol Beckwith & Angela Fisher 22 (main image).
Shutterstock: Clouston 21br, 32bl; Dana E. Fry 5; Andy Z. 4.
Still Pictures: K. Hennig 27

Jacket images: *Front:* **Photolibrary:** Franck Guiziou.
Back: **Shutterstock:** Clouston tr. **naturepl.com:** Eric Baccega tl.
All other images © Dorling Kindersley
For further information see: www.dkimages.com

Discover more at
www.dk.com

Contents

DK READERS

BEGINNING TO READ

1

Homes
Around the World

Written by Max Moore

DK

DK Publishing

Most of us live in houses or apartment buildings.

They are usually made of bricks or concrete.

But not all homes in the world are like this.
Some people live in unusual homes.

Would you like to live high
above the ground?
Some people who live in forests
and jungles build treehouses.

They use bamboo, vines, and
wood from the forest to make
their homes.

treehouse

Imagine you could go outside,
dig up some clay, and
use it to build a house.
People in very hot places
can do this.

The sun dries
the clay into strong
adobe bricks.

adobe

These cone-shaped mud-brick
homes are called beehive houses.
Their tall, cone-shaped roofs
help keep them cool inside.

All the hot air
rises to the top
of the house.

beehive house

What would it be like to live
on a lake?
Some people build their homes
on floating islands made of reeds.

They add a layer of fresh reeds
every few months.

reeds

Some fishermen build
wooden houses on stilts
over the water.
People walk along boardwalks
to get to stores, work, and school.

ramp

Would you like a house shaped
like a boat?
These wooden houses are
called tongkonans.
These are the homes of
the Toraja people.

tongkonan

Some houses have many carvings of plants and animals inside.

Have you ever moved to
a new house?
Some people move several times
every year.

They can fold up their houses
and set them up again
somewhere else.
These houses are covered with
  animal skins.

yurt

Straw tents can be moved, too. Straw is a light material but is also strong, warm, and doesn't let water in.

Straw can also be used to make the walls of homes that don't move.

Imagine living in a very cold place.
People used to build houses
from blocks of snow
to live in during the winter.

These igloos kept out the wind
and were warm inside.

In hot places, some people live
in houses carved into rocks.
Cave homes are warm
in the winter
and cool in
the summer.

Some people build houses
in ways that help the planet.

This house is heated only by
the sun.

This house is made from
old shipping containers.

These houses use less energy
and material than most homes.

Some people build silly houses
just for fun.
These homes are made
to look like a mound of bubbles
and an alien spaceship.

In the future, people may build their homes in other unusual ways.

Glossary

Adobe
a material made from dried earth and straw

Beehive house
a cone-shaped mud-brick house

Tongkonan
a wooden house shaped like a boat

Treehouse
a house built high up in the trees

Yurt
a round home that can be moved around

Index